JOHN CABOT

Please visit our web site at: www.worldalmanaclibrary.com
For a free color catalog describing World Almanac® Library's list of high-quality books
and multimedia programs, call 1-800-848-2928 (USA) or 1-800-387-3178 (Canada).
World Almanac® Library's fax: (414) 332-3567.

Library of Congress Cataloging-in-Publication Data

Bastable, Tony.
    John Cabot / by Tony Bastable.
        p. cm. — (Great explorers)
    Includes bibliographical references and index.
    Summary: Describes the life and voyages of the Italian-born explorer who claimed land
in the New World for England in 1497.
    ISBN 0-8368-5012-2 (lib. bdg.)
    ISBN 0-8368-5172-2 (softcover)
    1. Cabot, John, d. 1498?—Juvenile literature. 2. America—Discovery and exploration—
English—Juvenile literature. 3. North America—Discovery and exploration—English—Juvenile
literature. 4. Explorers—America—Biography—Juvenile literature. 5. Explorers—Great Britain—
Biography—Juvenile literature. 6. Explorers—Italy—Biography—Juvenile literature. [1. Cabot, John,
d. 1498? 2. Explorers. 3. America—Discovery and exploration—English.] I. Title. II. Great
explorers (Milwaukee, Wis.)
E129.C1B25   2003
970.01'7'092—dc21
    [B]   2003043299

This North American edition first published in 2004 by
World Almanac® Library
330 West Olive Street, Suite 100
Milwaukee, Wisconsin 53212 USA

This U.S. edition copyright © 2004 by World Almanac® Library.
Created with original © 2001 by Quartz Editions,
112 Station Road, Edgware HA8 7AQ, U.K.
Additional end matter copyright © 2004 by World Almanac® Library.

Series Editor: Tamara Green
World Almanac® Library editor: JoAnn Early Macken
World Almanac® Library designer: Melissa Valuch

The creators and publishers of this volume wish to thank the following for their kind permission to feature
illustration material:
Front cover: main image, Helen Jones/other images (from top to bottom) AKG/The Art Archive/Bridgeman Art
Library/Tony Stone Images/Stuart Brendon/AKG
Back cover: (from top to bottom) AKG/AKG/Newfoundland Historic Sites Association/Ancient Art & Architecture
Collection/Bridgeman Art Library
5 t Newfoundland Historic Sites Association/c Bridgeman Art Library/b AKG; 6 t, c, b AKG; 7 Helen Jones; 8
Bridgeman Art Library; 10 t Science Museum, Science & Society Picture Library/c Bridgeman Art Library/b The
Art Archive; 11 Science Museum, Science & Society Picture Library; 12-13 Stuart Brendon; 14 t Ancient Art &
Architecture Collection/c AKG; 16 t Mary Evans Picture Library/b AKG; 17 The Evening Telegram; 18 t AKG/b
Mary Evans Picture Library; 19 t Donald McCleod, Cabot Heritage Ltd/b AKG; 20 Mary Evans Picture Library;
21 from John Cabot and Newfoundland by Alan F. Williams; 22 t AKG/c The Art Archive/b Bridgeman Art
Library; 24 t AKG/b Bridgeman Art Library; p 25 t Bristol Record Office; 26 t Bridgeman Art Library/b
Newfoundland Historic Sites Association; 27 t AKG/b Bridgeman Art Library; 28 t Harvard College Library/b The
Evening Telegram; 30 The Evening Telegram; 31 t Mary Evans Picture Library; 32 t Mary Evans Picture Library/b
National Gallery of Art, Washington; 33 The Art Archive; 34 t Centre for Newfoundland Studies, Memorial
University of Newfoundland/b AKG; 35 c Bodleian Library, Oxford; 36 t AKG; 38 t Tony Stone Images/b
Bridgeman Art Library; 39 t Sonia Holiday Photographs/b Bridgeman Art Library; 40 t The Art Archive/c, b
Bridgeman Art Library; 42 t Mary Evans Picture Library/b The ArtArchive; 43 Helen Jones

Printed in Canada

1 2 3 4 5 6 7 8 9 07 06 05 04 03

JOHN CABOT

TONY BASTABLE

WORLD ALMANAC® LIBRARY

CONTENTS

INTRODUCTION

JOHN CABOT has the reputation of being one of history's greatest explorers, yet his life is filled with mystery. In fact, much of what he is said to have achieved is open to debate today.

This painting by Harold Goodridge, also shown on page 26, conveys the excitement of the first sighting of land by Cabot and his crew after they crossed the Atlantic in a ship built at the expense of the merchants of Bristol, England.

Without clocks as we know them, people had to rely on other instruments, such as those mentioned on pages 10 and 11, to tell time.

For information on how a replica of Cabot's ship, the *Matthew*, was built in England in 1997 to celebrate the five-hundredth anniversary of his arrival on the coast of Newfoundland, see pages 14-17.

No written records compiled by John Cabot himself remain, so everything we know about his fifteenth-century expeditions comes either from those who knew him personally or from others around at the time who reported what had been said of him.

A number of new theories have arisen as the result of the chance finding in 1955 of an important letter believed to have been sent to Christopher Columbus.

Cabot's reputation is based on expeditions from Bristol, England, westward across the North Atlantic, one of the coldest seas on Earth, to what according to the English spoken in his time was a "newe founde land." Cabot is widely credited with being the first European to set foot on North American soil, even though others, such as the Vikings, Leif Ericson, and St. Brendan, may have landed there centuries before him.

Yet Cabot was entirely unaware that he had in fact reached the mainland of this continent. Instead, he remained convinced that he was somewhere in Asia. His travels eventually led to the settlement of Newfoundland and other parts of Canada.

JOHN CABOT

MERCHANT SEAMAN

Cabot became a citizen of of Venice. He probably traveled around the city-state by gondola.

This painting shows Mecca, holy city of Islam, which Cabot is said to have visited disguised as a Muslim during the time he was a trader.

Cabot aimed to find a speedier route to Cathay (an old name for China) so he could trade more readily in exotic goods like embroidered silk (*right*).

Cabot has been honored as the first European to reach mainland North America. What was his motive, and who might have inspired him?

No official record exists of Cabot's date of birth, but it has been estimated at about 1450. At the time, Genoa, a city-state in what is now Italy, was one of the richest Mediterranean seaports. Many good sailors and successful merchants were among its inhabitants. Some historians believe Cabot was born in Genoa; other sources suggest he may have been born in Gaeta, near Naples.

We do know that by March 28, 1476, Cabot had been living in Venice for at least fifteen years. Historians are sure of this fact because on that date, Cabot was granted full citizenship of the city-state of Venice, which was known as "the queen of the Adriatic." To qualify for citizenship, a person had to have been living there for at least that length of time.

Although he was born Zuan, or (some sources say) Giovanni, Caboto, he was known outside of Italy by the English version of his name. From an early age, he was almost certainly as interested in commerce as he was in seafaring. There is evidence that during the 1480s, he ran a successful business, buying and selling property in Venice. By this time, he had married a Venetian woman named Mattea, with whom he had three sons — Lewis, Sebastian (who followed in his father's footsteps as an explorer), and Sancio.

Cabot is also known to have become involved in a legal dispute in 1484, a matter so costly that he had to borrow a large sum of money from his wife in order to settle it. He may have even had to start trading in foreign places to raise enough money to pay her back.

> *John Cabot is a man of good humor and a most expert mariner.*
> DE SONCINO

John Cabot seems to have been a practical man with an eye for business who dealt in goods and real estate before he went to sea.

King Ferdinand and Queen Isabella of Castile (*below*) refused to give their financial support to Cabot's planned voyage.

A man named Soncino recorded a conversation he had with Cabot in London in 1497. According to his report and other documents from the time, Cabot traveled extensively throughout the regions along the Mediterranean Sea as a trader from 1485 to 1490. Whether he acted on his own behalf or as an agent for a ship owner is not known.

It seems Cabot even traveled as far east as Mecca in what is now Saudi Arabia. Historians believe he must have disguised himself to make such a trip possible because only followers of the Islamic faith are officially allowed to enter the confines of the holy Muslim city.

MAKING A MOVE

In or about 1490, Cabot uprooted his family and moved to Valencia, Spain. There, drawing on his experience in real estate as well as his nautical and mapmaking skills, he put together detailed proposals for improvements to the Valencia harbor.

These ideas eventually reached the ear of King Ferdinand of Castile. Cabot had two meetings with the king in 1492. The king gave his seal of approval to Cabot's plan, but for unknown reasons, it was never adopted. Perhaps the money could not be raised. The plan may have met with another obstacle. We can only guess.

This map (*right*) shows the layout of Bristol, in southwest England, from where John Cabot set sail. Seafarers from Bristol had an excellent reputation and engaged in an enormous amount of international trade. Cabot speedily won their support for his proposed voyage across the Atlantic. The map dates from about 1581, but the city had not changed much since Cabot's time.

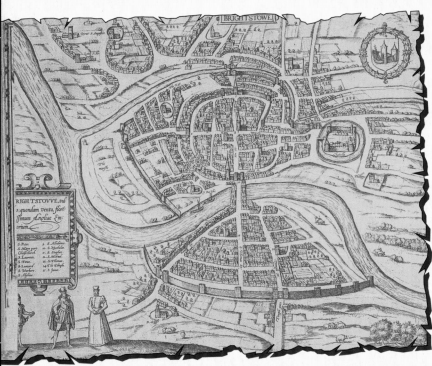

John Cabot spoke Italian, and no doubt, he also picked up a smattering of Spanish and Arabic during his early days as a merchant. After he moved to Bristol, he probably learned to speak English too.

In the long run, this incident did not really matter. Cabot had arrived in Valencia at one of the most exciting moments in European history. In April 1493, Christopher Columbus returned triumphantly to Spain. He was unaware he had actually landed in the West Indies. Instead, he believed that his fleet had discovered the eastern edge of Asia.

. . . the man who first opened North America to European civilization.

MOSES HARVEY
ON CABOT, 1897

Cabot probably did not entirely accept Columbus's claims, although he had been welcomed back to Spain as a hero. No one knows whether Cabot and Columbus, for all they had in common (both might have even been born in the same city) ever met to discuss the matter.

What does seem likely, however, is that Cabot was inspired by the voyages of Columbus and set out to prove him wrong.

A STRONG WILL

Cabot was certainly a determined man. After King Ferdinand and Queen Isabella of Castile refused to grant him financial backing for such a voyage, he went on to seek help from Portugal, another country with superb maritime traditions. Again, however, he failed to raise enough royal enthusiasm.

THIRD TIME LUCKY

Dogged perseverance eventually paid off, and his third attempt to raise financing proved successful. A group of merchants from Bristol, England, finally agreed to put up the necessary money for what must have seemed an ambitious voyage of discovery. Cabot would soon be on his way across the Atlantic, but there were surprises in store when his ship, the *Matthew*, landed.

TIME LINE

c. 1450
Cabot is born in Italy at about the time of Columbus's birth.

1485-90
Cabot travels to the eastern Mediterranean as a trader and visits Mecca.

1490
Cabot and his family move to Valencia, Spain, where he plans a new harbor.

1493
Cabot travels to Spain and Portugal but fails to raise funds for a transatlantic voyage.

1495
The Cabot family moves to Bristol, England.

1496
According to a letter found in 1955, King Henry VII grants permission for Cabot to cross the Atlantic in search of new lands. Cabot turns back because of bad weather, disputes with his crew, and lack of food.

1497
Cabot sails to Newfoundland on the *Matthew* and returns to Bristol in fifteen days.

1498
During Cabot's final expedition, one ship is damaged, and the other four are lost.

OVER THE OCEAN

LIBRI VII. TRACT II.

Early sailors used a quadrant (*above*), an instrument for navigating by the stars.

Hourglasses like this one (*right*) were regularly used onboard ships to measure time during long voyages. These devices were filled with sand.

This map of the globe (*right*) by the geographer Ptolemy dates from 1513. It does not accurately represent the positions of landmasses and seas as they are known today. Reliable maps were not available in medieval times. Mariners had to use simple navigational instruments and guesswork to find their way.

The late fifteenth century was a high point in exploration by sea. But most captains did not sail into uncharted waters for the adventure. Their aim was to make money.

A European who wanted to become rich during this period of history would almost certainly have traded in spices. Because there were no refrigerators, some spices were used to preserve meat or to mask the taste of it. Others, such as cloves, nutmeg, and cinnamon, were luxury items for the wealthy. Most spices grew far away in Asia, on the other side of the world from Europe. A journey to the Orient, whether overland or by sea, could take several months.

In 1453, the great city of Constantinople (now known as Istanbul) fell to the armies of the Ottoman Turks, and trade in spices was cut off.

By that time, it was generally accepted that the world was a sphere, not a flat disk balanced on the shell of a giant turtle, as many once thought. There had to be a westerly route to any destination on Earth.

Some people believed that a westerly route from Europe to Cathay, as China was known at the time, would be much shorter than traveling toward the east. From somewhere like Italy, however, a westerly route is, in fact, much longer. In the fifteenth century, many people thought the world was far smaller than it is now known to be.

THIS WAY OR THAT?

According to a fifteenth-century view of the world, all that was required to discover Japan and then Cathay was to sail west from Europe. An Italian from Florence named Toscanelli even produced a chart that showed the land known as Japan just three thousand miles to the west.

As it turned out, Toscanelli was correct in believing that a major landmass lay to the west. Although it was not Japan, previously unexplored territory did lie in that direction. European explorers were about to land on the continent of North America.

MAKING HEADWAY

At the end of the fifteenth century, there were few maps of places outside Europe. Those that did exist were mostly pure fantasy, based on legends of mythical islands. European sailors rarely lost sight of land, so they only had maps and charts of known coasts. How did sailors know where they were? They had fairly basic compasses to assess the course being steered, but these did not provide completely accurate readings. Latitude, the distance north or south of the equator, was calculated by using an instrument called a cross staff (right). On clear nights, a cross staff could measure the distance between the polestar and the horizon. Calculating longitude, the distance east or west, however, was much more difficult, if not impossible, before the invention of the chronometer in the eighteenth century by the Englishman John Harrison.

As a ship's crew gathered information, they recorded it in detailed logbooks known as rutters. This data was regarded as secret, and on certain ships, the penalty for divulging the content of the rutter was death.

The speed of a ship is measured in knots. A speed of ten knots, for example, means the ship sails the distance of ten nautical miles in one hour. A nautical mile is slightly longer than a land mile. It is equivalent to 1.15 land miles, or 1.85 kilometers.

GREENLAND

HUDSON BAY

NORTH ATLANTIC OCEAN

CANADA

LABRADOR

QUEBEC

GRAND BANKS

NEWFOUNDLAND

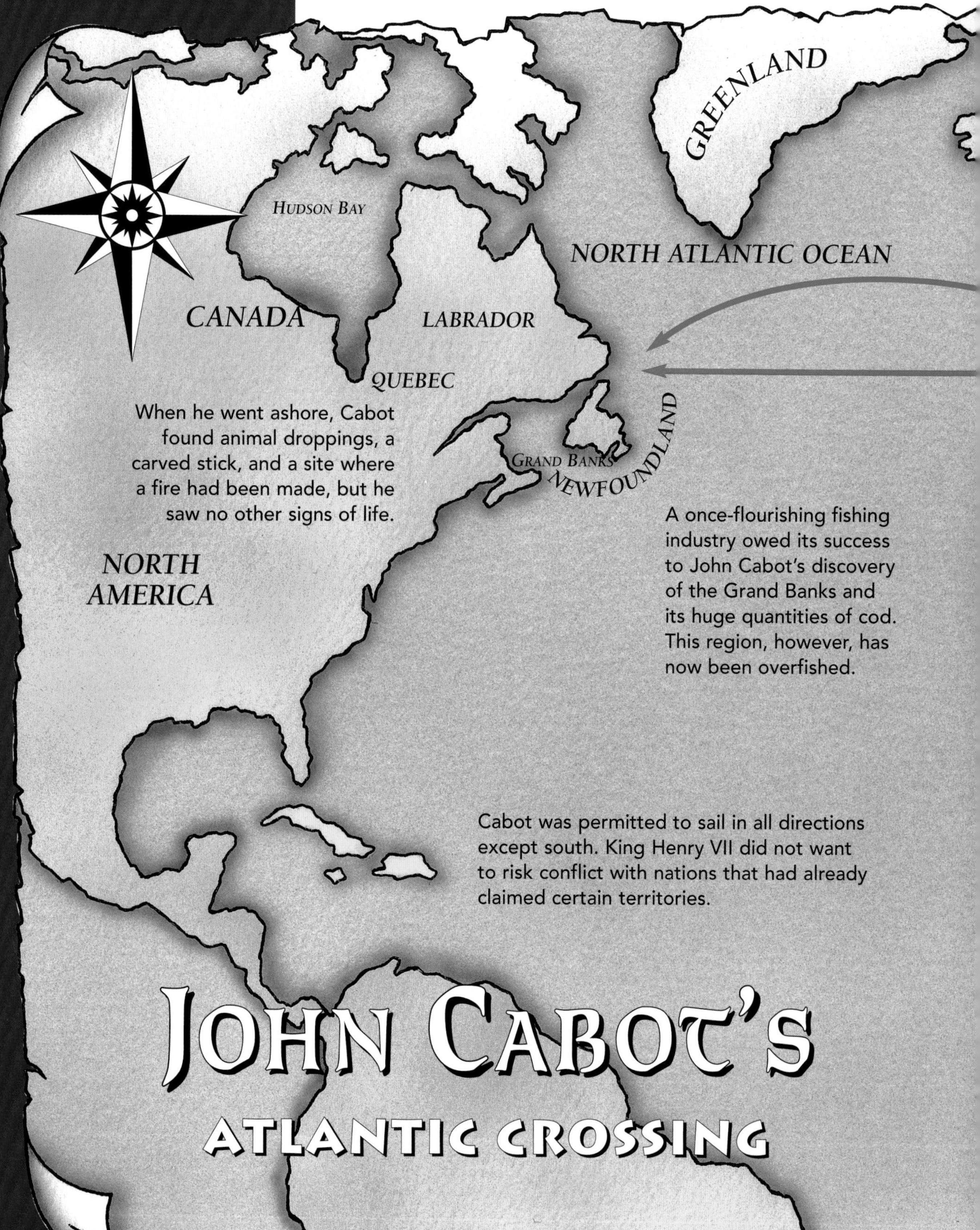

When he went ashore, Cabot found animal droppings, a carved stick, and a site where a fire had been made, but he saw no other signs of life.

NORTH AMERICA

A once-flourishing fishing industry owed its success to John Cabot's discovery of the Grand Banks and its huge quantities of cod. This region, however, has now been overfished.

Cabot was permitted to sail in all directions except south. King Henry VII did not want to risk conflict with nations that had already claimed certain territories.

JOHN CABOT'S
ATLANTIC CROSSING

ICELAND

EUROPE

Bristol

Venice

Genoa

Valencia
Lisbon

MOROCCO

MEDITERRANEAN SEA

Alexandria

EGYPT

SAUDI ARABIA

RED SEA

Mecca

One glance at a modern map shows that a direct sea route to the Orient in a westerly direction from Europe is blocked by the continent of North America. Cabot was not aware of the land, however; he thought the route would bring him to Cathay in record time.

KEY
Two possible routes

Cabot sought a new, speedier route to and from the Orient for the spice trade.

As a young man, John Cabot traded in goods from the East, such as silks and woven carpets.

John Cabot is said to have dressed as a Muslim in order to enter the holy city of Mecca, where only followers of the Islamic faith were allowed.

CANADA

LABRADOR

LABRADOR SEA

QUEBEC

CABOT STRAIT

NEWFOUNDLAND

BONAVISTA

CAPE BRETON ISLAND

St. John's

NEW BRUNSWICK

NOVA SCOTIA

ATLANTIC OCEAN

This inset map shows the positions of two places historians think were likely sites of Cabot's landfall in 1497 — Cape Breton Island and Cape Bonavista.

VERY FINE VESSELS

Most fifteenth-century ships were built to carry cargo, like this argosy from Venice, Italy (*above*), pictured in stained glass.

Explorers embarking on overseas voyages required reliable ships. The *Matthew*, a caravel, seems to have performed well.

This illustration (*above*), intended to show the building of Noah's ark, dates from 1493 and features the construction of a typical European seagoing vessel of the period, not one of biblical times.

In northern Europe in the fourteenth century, most of the ships tied up in the ports were simple crafts known as cogs. A cog had just one mast and a single square sail.

Two very different kinds of ships crossed the waters of the Mediterranean at that time. One was the galley, a two-masted vessel that carried sails but also relied on oarsmen for speed and maneuvering. Slaves were usually chained to the oars. The galley was the principal war vessel of those days. Other types of vessels, which

were designed for maximum cargo space, had two huge rudders at the sides instead of the rear.

The galley remained in use in the Mediterranean for some time to come. By the fifteenth century, however, two other designs of sailing ship from northern and southern Europe had merged to produce a carrack. The carrack was a large vessel with up to five masts that could carry a huge amount of cargo, but it was very slow. When faced with a headwind, the captain had little choice but to lower his sails, heave to (bring the ship to a stop), and wait for the wind to swing around to a more favorable direction.

The Arabs solved this sort of problem with the dhow,

This four-cent Canadian stamp (*left*) shows the *Matthew*. The caption appears in both French and English.

which is used to this day. The dhow is a fast ship with triangular sails that make it possible to sail almost directly into a headwind. This means that the dhow can continue moving forward slowly in conditions that would force other ships to a halt. Nevertheless, the dhow usually faces gentler weather than that in the Atlantic.

The inspiration for the breakthrough that was to

> " *The original Matthew was built from English oak, the preferred timber of medieval ship-builders.* "

transform European ships came from a quiet, studious man who did not sail to faraway places himself, Prince Henry of Portugal, known to history as Henry the Navigator. He was a highly educated person who wrote scientific works on astronomy and enjoyed debates with other scientists, mapmakers, master mariners, and ships' pilots.

Henry the Navigator also established the first school for navigation in Europe at Sagres, in the Algarve region of southern Portugal. Here, Henry's experts worked on the type of ship that was to become the vessel of choice for such explorers as John Cabot and Christopher Columbus.

A NEW DESIGN

The caravel, as it was called, combined the sailing advantages of the Arab dhow with the solid construction of the carrack. The caravel was smaller than the carrack and could float in shallower waters, making it ideal for exploring unknown territories. With its hemp or canvas lateen (triangular) sails, it could sail close to the wind. Caravels later carried square sails, too, for easier sailing in the trade winds of the open oceans.

A caravel like the *Matthew*, Cabot's ship, would have been about 75 feet (22.9 meters) long and perhaps 20-25 feet (6.1-7.6 m) wide. It would have had two decks. A very large hatch opening into the hold would have made the lower deck a very restricted, narrow structure that resembled a sort of platform running all around the inside of the ship.

Most of these ships also carried some form of armament, usually cannons.

CARGO

There are no records remaining to show whether John Cabot and his crew took with them goods for trading on the voyage of 1497. It would be surprising if they did not, however, because Cabot's whole aim was to find a new route to Cathay, a haven for silks, precious stones, and spices. On the fatal voyage of 1498, however, we know that Cabot took along coarse cloth, capes, lace, and other small items supplied by the merchants of Bristol in the hope that opportunities for trading might arise. As far as we know, they did not. The explorers would surely have had ample supplies of food onboard. John Cabot would have learned a lesson from a voyage in 1496 that supposedly failed not only because of bad weather conditions but also because there was not enough food and drink to satisfy the crew. This time, they were no doubt well stocked with pickled meat. The bread they took along, however, would turn moldy and worm ridden before the round trip was completed. By law, sailing ships of this time were required to have at least one cat onboard to kill rats that might otherwise contaminate the food.

ALL ABOARD

The crew of a caravel about the size of the *Matthew* would probably have included a number of specialists in addition to the regular seamen. Besides the captain, the first mate, and a cook, a carpenter would almost certainly have been onboard to do any necessary on-the-spot repairs.

A cooper would have been employed to build and repair barrels — a highly essential job at that time. The barrel was the only way to transport supplies of fresh water.

The *Matthew*, which might have been named in honor of Cabot's wife, Mattea, might also have carried a specialist gunner and a barber, whose job was not only to shave and trim beards but to act as a surgeon as well.

A priest would often have been a member of a ship's company. These were pious times, and men of religion were required to pray for calm weather and a safe return. A total of eighteen men made up Cabot's crew.

Unfortunately, no fifteenth-century caravel has survived to this day. Imagine, then, the problems facing the designer when, just a few years ago, it was decided to try to re-create Cabot's ship, the *Matthew*, to celebrate the five-hundredth anniversary of his 1497 Atlantic voyage. Colin Mudie, an experienced yacht designer, was faced with the challenge. He knew it would be impossible to build an exact replica.

Instead, he decided to set the dimensions of the vessel at an overall length of nearly 70 feet (21.3 m) and a beam, or width, of about 20 feet (6.1 m). This provided the ship with sufficient carrying capacity for a replica fifteenth-century expedition that would probably have lasted about six months. The ship also needed enough space for replacement sails and rigging, extra timber to make running repairs and seal possible leaks, and sufficient food to have sustained Cabot and his crew.

The original *Matthew* was built in Bristol out of English oak, and so was the new vessel. The exception was the keel, built of African opepe because no oak tree could be found that was large enough to provide a single piece of wood fifty feet long. The builders also decided to use aluminum and bronze bolts in place of iron nails, which tend to rust.

Modern safety regulations demanded that this ship be fitted with a diesel engine and up-to-date navigational aids. Meanwhile, hygiene was assured by the installation on the new *Matthew* of hot and cold showers — something unimaginable to a fifteenth-century sailor.

Decisions also had to be made about the type of sails.

Mudie decided Cabot would have opted for square sails in addition to the lateen type, because he expected to be sailing with following winds, for which square rigging is more suited.

Finally, in early May 1997, the reconstruction was ready. The twentieth-century vessel made the trip from Bristol to Newfoundland successfully and arrived to be greeted with a huge welcome and widespread publicity when it landed. Indeed, when asked how the ship had sailed, one of the crew replied: "Like a pig!"

The modern *Matthew's* sails are furled in a photograph taken in 1997 (*left*). The ship was built to be as much like the original as possible. Only the keel was made of a different type of wood.

A photographer from a Newfoundland newspaper, the *Evening Telegram*, took this aerial shot of the modern *Matthew* while it was at sea with the sails of its three masts unfurled and billowing in the wind.

Tunne is an Old English word for a large barrel with a capacity of just over 250 gallons (946 liters). The size of ships eventually became rated by the number of such barrels for which there was space onboard, and today the original word lives on in the nautical term *tonnage*.

This decorative brass casing (*below right*) holds an astrolabe. These instruments were devised more than two thousand years ago. They first came to Europe from Spain during the twelfth century. They helped with navigation by showing how the sky looked at a certain time.

SOME LASTING RIDDLES

A number of unsolved mysteries surround John Cabot's voyages. How many times did he try to reach North America?

This illustration from a modern collectors' card set shows the *Matthew* shortly after setting sail from Bristol on May 2, 1497.

Until recently, it was thought that John Cabot only made two trips out of Bristol, one in 1497 and one in 1498, the expedition from which he did not return. In the mid-1950s, however, a mysterious letter was discovered. Before that time, it had been hidden in an ancient Spanish library.

The letter, addressed to "the Lord Grand Admiral," was almost certainly written to Christopher Columbus by a man who used the pseudonym of John Day.

A citizen of Bristol, John Day also had close contact with Spain. He may have been a Spanish spy; no one knows for certain now.

From this letter, historians discovered that Cabot is likely to have made three journeys from the port of Bristol, not just two. Even more intriguing is the fact that the first trip seems to have been made in 1496, a year earlier than the voyage for which John Cabot is now most famous.

> 66 *They spent about one month discovering the coast [of Newfoundland]. . . then they returned to Europe in fifteen days.* 99
>
> FROM JOHN DAY'S LETTER TO COLUMBUS, 1497

Nobody knows the real purpose of this earlier voyage or even whether it actually took place. Historians have suggested it may have been some sort of trial run to test out the equipment or the *Matthew* itself.

RETURN TO PORT

Whatever the reason, however, the voyage was not a success. As Day's letter states, "He went with one ship, his crew confused him, he was short of supplies and ran into bad weather, and he decided to turn back."

The following year, however, Cabot had far better luck. The *Matthew*, possibly with Cabot's second son, Sebastian, onboard as a member of the crew, left the port of Bristol in May 1497.

Cabot's exact course is unknown, but the best guess is that he sailed to the northwest. This seems logical because the crews of shipping vessels would have been familiar with Icelandic waters from previous fishing expeditions.

Once ashore, Cabot sent out a search party. But the men were nervous about venturing too far inland. According to Day's letter, they "believed the land to be inhabited," so they "did not advance beyond the shooting distance of a crossbow."

John Cabot sailed west in 1496. It is not known how far north his route took him. He may have had trouble navigating through ice floes like these (*below*).

Cabot and his crew first landed off the North American continent at a place he called St. John's Island. He gave a different name to the land he first saw after crossing the Atlantic — Prima Terra Vista, which means "land first seen" in Spanish.

MATTERS OF FAITH

Religion was very much a part of everyday life for people in the fifteenth and sixteenth centuries, especially for those Christians onboard ships who believed they were entrusting their fate to the Almighty. They prayed to the "Star of the Sea," the Virgin Mary, for protection from danger. It is known for certain that priests accompanied Cabot's fleet on his final voyage in 1498. Ironically, no one returned from this voyage. They may have been lost at sea.

REGULAR DEVOTIONS

Writings left by Cabot's son, Sebastian, reveal that faith played an important part onboard ship. For example, it was required that "morning and evening prayer, with the common services appointed by the King's Majestie, be read daily by the chaplain or some other person learned."

GRATEFUL TO GOD

Thanks were regularly given to God for successful voyages of discovery at that time. When Cabot landed in North America, he marked the event not only by naming the place where he landed after St. John, whose day it was, but also by erecting a cross and the banners of the King of England, from where he had sailed, the Pope (head of the Roman Catholic Church), and St. Mark of Venice.

While Columbus was committed to converting to Christianity those he met in newly discovered territory, Cabot seems to have been more interested in the commercial side of exploration. Even so, he would most likely have followed church teachings carefully.

Both before and after meals onboard, the priest would no doubt have said prayers for the ship's company, thanking God on everyone's behalf for adequate supplies of food and water.

Prayers were probably also said for the sponsors of such a voyage, for royalty, and for the families the sailors had left behind and would not see until they returned months, or even years, later. As far as historians can tell, sailors' wives never accompanied them on such voyages.

Sailors did not have individual prayer books at that time, so they

This fifteenth-century illustration shows a merchant vessel being attacked by a devil but enjoying the divine protection of the Almighty.

would have relied on the ship's priest to speak for them while they stood in respectful silence.

Strict rules of behavior were also laid down onboard ship so that God would not be offended. Sebastian Cabot, for example, ordered that "no blaspheming of God, or detestable swearing be used." Orders like this survived for a long time, and seamen were expected to obey them rigidly.

BAD OMENS

But sailors of the fifteenth century also held some superstitions. They believed, for example, that no one should ever destroy a printed page in case it might have come from a Bible. They thought no ship should ever sail on a Friday because Jesus was crucified on that day of the week. Knives crossed on a table or spilled salt were believed to bring bad luck.

The captain was allowed to whistle onboard, but no one else was. Even the captain was only permitted to do so when he needed to "whistle up a wind."

Most extraordinary of all, a seaman who happened to hear someone sneeze on his left side as he boarded a ship could be convinced that the vessel was doomed and might even refuse to sail on it.

A sailor's objections were generally accepted in spite of the regulations. Indeed, it seems that superstition ruled onboard a fifteenth-century European ship almost as much as the Christian religion.

SIGNS OF HABITATION

On land, Cabot and his crew found plenty of signs of life, although they did not encounter any actual inhabitants. They located a well-worn track, the remains of a fire, felled trees, and a stick "half a yard long, pierced at both ends, carved and painted."

As for the place itself, it was heavily wooded with trees "of the kind masts are made," and the weather was warm. Cabot and his men spent an hour or so looking around. They refilled their barrels with fresh water from a stream, and then they returned to their ship. Surprisingly, it seems to have been the only time Cabot and his crew stepped onto North American soil.

No one knows exactly where Cabot landed, either. Perhaps it was as far south as the coast of what is now the state of Maine or, more likely, hundreds of miles farther north near Cape Bauld in what is now Newfoundland. Cape Bauld lies almost exactly on the same latitude as a place called Dursey Head on the extreme west coast of Ireland, which was well known to local mariners of that time.

Another great mystery concerns the length of time it took the *Matthew* to cross the Atlantic Ocean. One record claims that it took the vessel just fifteen days to get back to Bristol. If this is true, the ship must have completed the journey at an average speed of around five knots, very fast going at the time. Whatever the case, King Henry VII was impressed and presented Cabot with a reward. He even became known as the "Great Admiral." As a Venetian of the time described Cabot's popularity, "These English run after him like mad."

This woodcut of a sea monster, which was believed in medieval times to inhabit the North Atlantic, was made as late as 1550.

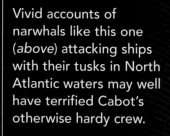

Vivid accounts of narwhals like this one (*above*) attacking ships with their tusks in North Atlantic waters may well have terrified Cabot's otherwise hardy crew.

In some historical documents, the name Zuam Talbot is used with reference to John Cabot. This may have been an English version of his name. In Italian records, meanwhile, he is named Zoane or Giovanni Caboto. In other chronicles of his travels, his surname is given as Gaboto.

ROYAL AND MERCHANT ALLIES

Without the help of backers, Cabot would never have been able to sail. Who supported him financially and encouraged him?

King Henry VII, seen here in front of a map of the east coast of North America, granted letters patent to Cabot.

King Henry VII had a reputation for being careful with money. He hoped to gain financially from Cabot's voyages. The testoon (*right*) was first minted during his reign. It was worth about twelve pence, or pennies.

As a former merchant and trader himself, Cabot would have known how best to present his proposals as an exciting opportunity for profit. This was just the sort of thing King Henry VII of England liked to hear. Such was the King's character that if he had been born today as an ordinary citizen instead of a king, he might have had a bright future as the chairman of a large company, as an accountant, or perhaps as a tax collector.

In anything to do with money, Henry VII was one of the shrewdest and canniest men — perhaps even the meanest — ever to sit on the throne of England.

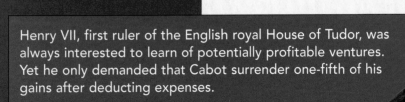

Henry VII, first ruler of the English royal House of Tudor, was always interested to learn of potentially profitable ventures. Yet he only demanded that Cabot surrender one-fifth of his gains after deducting expenses.

> " *We give and grant . . . to our well-beloved John Cabot . . . full and free authority . . . to sail to all parts, regions and coasts of the eastern, western and northern sea, under our banners . . .* "
>
> KING HENRY VII

A classic example of his ability to squeeze money out of his subjects became known as "Morton's fork."

John Morton was Archbishop of Canterbury and also Henry's chancellor, or secretary, in the early years of Henry's reign. The two men together worked out an unanswerable argument for raising money. Any man who was well dressed and had many servants was clearly rich, so he could afford to pay more taxes. A more modest-looking man must have been careful with his money and probably saved lots of it. So he could afford to pay even more taxes!

Like a spider sitting in the middle of his web, Henry noticed everything. Shortly after he came to the throne, he visited Bristol and found that merchants there claimed trade was very poor. But Henry spotted that their wives were elegantly dressed, suggesting business was not as bad as they claimed.

He increased the taxes to be paid by these merchants. If a profit was to be made, King Henry VII found a way to make it.

A HIGH PRICE

England was just about the most distant customer for the eastern spice trade, so the price there was even higher than the astronomical levels reached in Mediterranean markets. When he granted Cabot an audience, the king would therefore have been impressed with the potential profits to be made from Cabot's proposed new route to the Orient. Christopher Columbus had initially approached Henry for backing but was turned down. The king was not about to make the same mistake again. Besides, Cabot's plan appealed to him because Earth's curvature suggested that the distance to the east coast of Asia would be shorter in more northern latitudes.

TEAM SPIRIT

● Cabot's crew would have had certain rights and duties as set out in a document known as the Laws of Rhodes and Oleron. These were surprisingly democratic and even regulated the number of meals to which the men were entitled.

● Big decisions were made by a majority vote. The captain could always override the result, but he would do so at his peril.

● The laws made something else clear, too. "A ship's company are entitled to refuse to undertake a voyage which will jeopardize their lives," they clearly stated. Cabot would have kept this in mind at all times.

● To maintain good conduct among his crew, a sea captain was allowed to strike a single blow at any sailor whose behavior was out of line. After that, however, the culprit could defend himself against such corporal punishment.

● These laws helped to maintain a sense of comradeship onboard ship as well as providing for the men's welfare so that for the most part they remained in good spirits.

King Henry VII and the merchants of Bristol knew of the earlier voyages of Columbus, shown about to set sail in 1492 (*above*) with sponsorship from the Castilian crown. Henry and the merchants supported Cabot's voyage to find a new route to the Orient.

This illustration from *Narrative and Critical History of America* shows cod being caught and dried. The merchants of Bristol and other European seafarers benefited financially from cod for many centuries.

There was also, King Henry VII thought, still a good chance that an English expedition would reach Asia and start trading with Cathay before the Spanish arrived. But what was even more appealing about Cabot's proposal was that he was prepared to sail, as they said in those days, "on his own proper charges." In other words, Henry would not have to pay a penny.

FAVORABLE TERMS

Anyone hoping to discover new lands required official permission. The documents, or letters patent, were expensive to prepare. The person who requested permission was responsible for having them drawn up, so once again, Henry avoided having to make a financial contribution.

The King's letters patent, issued on March 5, 1496,

gave John Cabot and his three sons — Sebastian, Lewis, and Sancio — "full and free authoritie, leave and power to sayle to all partes, countreys and seas, of the East, of the West, and of the North, under our banners and ensignes, with five ships . . . upon their own proper costes and charges . . . to seek out and finde whatsoever iles, countreyes, regions or provinces of the heathen and infidelles, whatsoever they bee, and in what part of the world soever they be, whiche before this time have been unknowen to all Christians."

Note, however, that no permission was granted for them to sail south. Through a papal decree, known as the Treaty of Tordesillas, the Caribbean had previously been divided up between Spain and Portugal. So this region had already been

explored to some extent by Christian Europeans. Henry VII was wary and did not want any mariner on a voyage of discovery for England to risk conflict with these powerful seafaring nations.

Many people believe that the word America comes from the name of Columbus's navigator, Amerigo Vespucci. It might actually have come from the name Richard Amerike. Amerike was a Bristol merchant who was one of the principal backers of Cabot's voyages.

Among the merchants in this image is William Spencer (*center left*), seen swearing in his successor as Lord Mayor of Bristol.

In return for the letters patent, the King was to receive twenty percent of any profits, which was a very fair arrangement. The Bristol merchants who backed Cabot's expedition were party to an excellent deal, too.

> **News from England . . . His Majesty sent out a Venetian who is a very good mariner.**
>
> DUKE OF MILAN, 1497

The letters patent also made it plain that all goods brought back to England from any voyages undertaken to such new lands by Cabot and his heirs would be free of customs duties and that they could only be landed in the port of Bristol.

Henry was extremely pleased with the results of Cabot's voyages. The king awarded Cabot a pension of £20 sterling a year, which was a large sum of money at that time. The pension continued to be paid until September 1499, after Cabot disappeared on his final voyage.

The £20 sterling had not unduly bothered King Henry. Typically, he ordered it paid out of the customs revenues of the Port of Bristol, so once again, it cost him nothing personally.

A WRONG HUNCH

King Henry must have been very excited when he heard what Cabot had to say about the 1497 expedition. The king would have sensed that vast amounts of profit were likely to be made.

Acting on that hunch, he did something that might have been out of character. He took what he probably thought was not much of a gamble and volunteered to provide and provision one of the five ships to sail on a new expedition the following year, 1498. This time, however, Henry lost out on a financial deal. John Cabot and the King's expensive ship were never seen again.

Sebastian Cabot has been wrongly pictured on this stamp with wording about his father, John.

TAKING GREAT RISKS

In medieval times, sailing into an uncharted ocean could have involved considerable danger. On some voyages, the chances of a safe return were remote.

This woodcut symbolizes the dangers St. Brendan, an Irish monk, faced when he sailed across Atlantic waters in a primitive boat hundreds of years before Cabot's voyages. Sailing out of the Bristol Channel would have been risky because of the strong tides.

Most of Cabot's crew would have been from Bristol because the port had a long tradition of sailing in northern waters. Also, the expedition was backed by local merchants who would have preferred a local crew. It must have seemed an unusual arrangement to Cabot, who had previously sailed in the Mediterranean.

There, crews tended to be more cosmopolitan. But a recent account reveals that he was accompanied on his first voyage by a friend from Burgundy, France, and a barber from Genoa, Italy, where Cabot may have been born. That means he would have had at least one companion to speak with in his native language.

This modern work by artist Harold Goodridge, painted in 1947, is called "John Cabot Sighting Cape Bonavista." Historians think this region is one of the places where the explorer might have made landfall in 1497, but no one has ever proven the precise location.

Although most voyages were relatively routine, sailors in those times survived some remarkable trips, given the conditions in which they worked and lived. Each sailor came onboard carrying a small sea chest containing a wooden food bowl, a leather mug, and one change of clothing.

> *The chances of the Matthew getting across and back were a great deal shorter than of the Apollo reaching and returning from the moon.*
> PRINCE PHILIP, 1997, BUCKINGHAM PALACE, LONDON

A sailor's clothing included a coarse serge gown with a hood to keep the spray off his face, loose trousers, and long woolen stockings. Sailors did have leather shoes, but they were not worn on deck. Men went barefoot there so they were less likely to slip over.

Unless weather conditions were truly awful, sailors rolled themselves up in blankets and slept on deck.

At the end of the nineteenth century, a brass plaque was commissioned by the Royal Society of Canada to mark John Cabot's successes four hundred years earlier. Since he reached its eastern shore, the land now known as Canada has extended to the far Pacific coast.

They must have always been wet, or at least damp, and covered in a thin layer of salt. When conditions became really bad, they were allowed to go below.

Sanitary arrangements were minimal. The best way for a sailor to relieve himself was over the bow (the forward part of the ship), but this was not always possible in bad weather.

The alternative was to use the ship's hold. After days at sea, the stench must have been unbearable.

If the weather warmed up, cockroaches and other insects would appear. Sailors also faced a constant threat of being bitten by rats, but at least their numbers were controlled by the ship's cat.

In 1492, Martin Behaim, shown with colleagues, completed the oldest surviving globe. Cabot and Columbus shared many of his ideas, but neither ever met him.

This detail from an illustrated map of the east coast of North America shows ships in combat. It was fortunate that Cabot had no conflicts at sea.

The designer of the replica *Matthew* (*below*) was lucky. In 1982, Henry VII's sunken flagship, the Mary Rose, built ten years after Cabot's craft, was raised. It gave useful clues to fifteenth-century ship structure.

What supplies would have been brought along? There would have been lots of beer — a typical allowance was at least a gallon a day per man. (Mediterranean sailors were entitled to similarly generous amounts of wine.)

Although water was easy to obtain when it rained, it was drunk onboard only as a last resort after the liquor ran out.

Food was prepared in a cook-box, which looked like a small shed. It was usually located on deck near the bow. Inside the cook-box, a fire was built on a thick base of sand or earth. In rough weather, however, the food was served cold. No one wanted to take the risk of a stray piece of glowing wood being blown from the cook-box by the wind and setting fire to the ship.

FRUGAL FARE

The staple diet onboard was based on meat and fish, both of which would start to rot after a couple of weeks at sea if they were not salted enough to preserve them. Bread was baked onboard whenever the weather allowed it.

Flour for baking bread and ship's biscuits was kept in the driest part of the vessel, but before long, it would become infested with weevils and worms.

At the beginning of every voyage, there were no doubt chickens, goats, and other livestock onboard to supply the crew with eggs and milk. But some of these animals may not have survived for long at sea and would have been cooked and eaten.

If behavior onboard ever

> **It was against all odds, too, that . . . a keen yachtsman, donated £1.5 million for the building of a replica ship in 1997.**

got out of control, a number of punishments could be employed. Offenders could be dunked, bound to the capstan or the mainmast with a bucket of shot around their necks, or keelhauled. Keelhauling involved pulling them down one side of the ship on a rope. They were hauled across the bottom of

the ship's hull (across the keel) and back up the other side. For much of the event, the culprits were underwater. Because ships' hulls are often covered in rough barnacles and razor-sharp shells, they ended up in a sorry state. For very serious offenses, a guilty crew member could even be executed.

Severe punishments were almost certainly not as common as some people believe today. For most of a typical voyage, the men simply performed their regular duties.

BELIEVE IT OR NOT?

The fact that what John Cabot had to tell about his voyage of 1497 was even taken at face value is somewhat surprising. As a letter from London to the Duke of Milan, Italy, written in December of that year, explains, however, ". . . as a foreigner and poor, he [Cabot] would probably not have been believed had it not been that his companions, practically all Englishmen and from Bristol, testified he spoke the truth."

WEATHER REPORT

One unusual thing about early accounts of Cabot's 1497 voyage is that they do not mention bad weather. Normally, mariners would expect to find fog around the islands off the coast of Newfoundland. Icebergs also must have made navigation difficult. It has been suggested that Cabot and his crew may have conspired not to mention the weather so that future expeditions to the region would not be cut short. John Day wrote that a gale struck a couple of days before Cabot's landfall on June 24. It may have caused panic onboard.

CABOT'S FINAL VOYAGE

A statue of John Cabot guards a government building in St. John's, Newfoundland.

John Cabot set sail from Bristol again in 1498, but as far as we know, he never returned. Clues suggest that he may have explored more extensively than ever.

John Cabot left no diaries or ships' logs, and no detailed accounts exist from the time of his travels. Unlike Ferdinand Magellan, he had no loyal diarist to record his travels, and it was not even until as recently as the mid-twentieth century that historians discovered he had probably made three voyages instead of just two.

Very little is known about this recently discovered early voyage. Its possible outcome, however, is regarded by historians as one of the most fascinating enigmas of the late fifteenth century.

By 1498, the English king, as well as the merchants of London and Bristol, were eager to invest in another expedition.

Cabot's Tower on Signal Hill in St. John's, Newfoundland (*left*), was used by Marconi to send the first transatlantic radio signal in 1901.

The idea was that Cabot should sail west as before but then turn south and keep sailing. In due course, it was thought, he would reach Cipango (Japan). To the east of Japan, they believed, lay the coast of Cathay and other lands ruled by the Great Khan, as Marco Polo had described.

A small fleet of five ships was assembled. The ships were loaded with all kinds of merchandise, including lace, cloth, caps, trinkets, earrings, and necklaces, as well as highly decorated swords and other weapons, in case any opportunities for trade arose. Not long after they left, however, one of the ships turned up at an Irish port, apparently badly damaged in a gale.

Of the remaining four ships, their crews, and their leader, nothing is known for certain.

One possibility is that the ship sailing back to Ireland was the only surviving vessel, and all the others had been wrecked. A key record of the time states that all five ships were missing. Of course, any ship sailing into unknown waters would have been considered missing unless and until it turned up somewhere.

We also know that Cabot's fleet sailed with enough food to last at least a year, so no one would have worried unduly if the ships had not turned up within that time.

The other problem with the lost-at-sea theory is that there is no known precedent for all the ships on an Atlantic expedition to have been lost in a storm.

A SORRY END?

If the rest of the fleet was not lost after all, where did the ships end up? They may, of course, have returned to a British or European port, either alone or as a group, not having reached their intended destination.

Bad weather is a hazard for all sailors, and it is by no means a sign of failure meriting loss of face to run into a storm. In such circumstances, a sensible decision would have been to turn back and repair any damage. No doubt, the merchants who backed this voyage would have been pleased to see at least four of the five ships return with their cargo intact and their crews still alive.

Some people still believe that Cabot returned to England and later died there. Most historians find it unlikely, however, that the four ships returned to Europe.

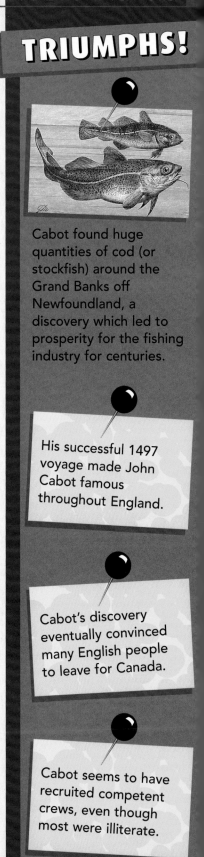

TRIUMPHS!

Cabot found huge quantities of cod (or stockfish) around the Grand Banks off Newfoundland, a discovery which led to prosperity for the fishing industry for centuries.

His successful 1497 voyage made John Cabot famous throughout England.

Cabot's discovery eventually convinced many English people to leave for Canada.

Cabot seems to have recruited competent crews, even though most were illiterate.

Built, Anno 1110
Demolished 1656

The south prospect of part of the Castle of Bristoll
Avon flu

John Cabot may have been honored after his return from the voyage of 1497 by local and London merchants at magnificent Bristol Castle (*above*), which was destroyed in 1656. He probably did not return to Europe from the voyage he made in 1498.

This detail from a Flemish painting, "The Martyrdom of St. Catherine," shows a caravel drying out at low tide and another being built with scaffolding. Regular cleaning and repairs were essential to keep such vessels seaworthy.

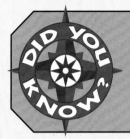

The sailing of the replica *Matthew* in 1997 coincided with the sighting of a comet. In medieval times, this phenomenon was believed to herald disaster. If Cabot saw such an omen, he might have waited a while before going to sea.

FURTHER POSSIBILITIES

The idea that Cabot may have kept sailing and exploring the east coast of North America is a likely possibility.

Three key pieces of evidence support this version of events. In 1499, the Spanish appointed an unpleasant character, Alonso de Hojeda, to follow up Columbus's third expedition. It was he who named the South American country of Venezuela — literally "Little Venice" — when he saw huts built on wooden poles in the water. (Venice, Italy, is crossed by many canals.) Somewhere in Venezuela, according to one report, "it is certain that Hojeda in his first voyage encountered certain Englishmen. . . ."

Indeed, the King of Spain awarded Hojeda a parcel of land on Hispaniola (the island that includes the Dominican Republic and Haiti) for "the stopping of the English."

If this is true, then the explorers' fate would have been sealed. Hojeda would most likely have put them to death in order to cancel out any claims to newly discovered lands. But the work of mapmaker Juan de la Cosa, who accompanied Hojeda, also comes into play.

When de la Cosa returned to Spain in 1500, he drafted the first map to show the entire continent of North America. Along the coastline, the mapmaker drew symbols of flags with the words "sea discovered by the English."

Because de la Cosa was a Spaniard, it certainly would not have been in his interests to make this up. Spain had laid claim to all this territory. Could he

have talked with some of Cabot's surviving crew while in Venezuela?

The next clue we have is the most intriguing. In 1501, the Portuguese explorer Gaspar Corte-Real sailed on his second expedition. He landed somewhere on the east coast of North America. His landfall is likely to have been somewhere in what is now Nova Scotia.

When he returned to Portugal, he brought with him seven Native Americans. Curiously, one boy had a pair of silver earrings that were recognized as being Venetian. The captives also had a broken Italian gilt sword.

Cabot would probably not have left these objects on his 1497 expedition because he was only ashore for a few hours, and he met with no local people. If he left the objects, it must have been in 1498 or later.

If this story is accurate, then John Cabot and his crew could have settled after their third voyage not in Venezuela but much farther north in the territory of Nova Scotia. We may never know for sure.

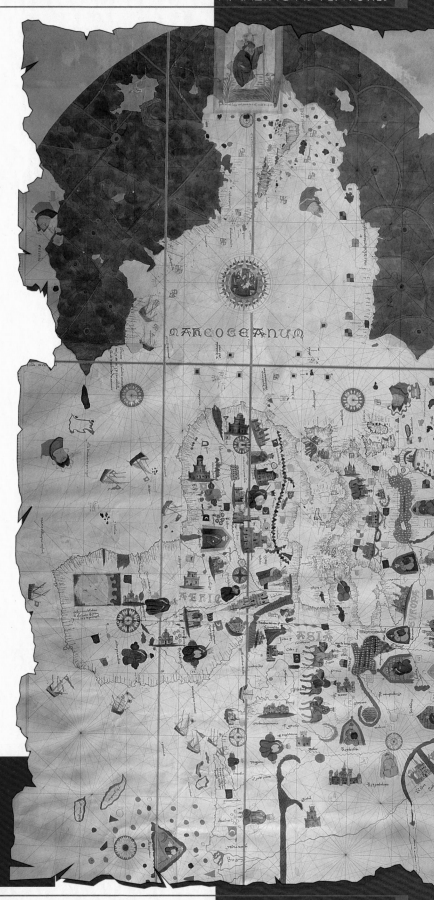

Columbus's pilot, Juan de la Cosa, made this map (*right, aligned east-west*) in 1500. It shows the Old World and the New World but is very sketchy and has faded over the years.

NEW FOUND LAND

The land labeled *Terra Nova* ("new land" in Latin) and the islands to the south of it on this map from 1556 (*above*) represent Newfoundland. To the west is the landmass that first came to be known as New France (in Latin, *Nuova Francia*). The chart was made by Italian Jacomia di Gastaldi.

At a custom house quay, or landing place, ships arrive with imported goods (*right*). In Cabot's time and since then, items from other parts of the world were taxed. Henry VII said in Cabot's letters patent that Cabot, his sons, and his heirs "shall be free and exempt from all payment of customs on all . . . goods and merchandise that they may bring back with them from those places thus newly discovered."

John Cabot not only succeeded in reaching territory new to Europeans, he also came across rich fishing grounds. But was he really the first to discover them?

It is possible, some historians think, that as trade in fish between Europe and Iceland increased during the Middle Ages, fishing boat crews had often seen the east coast of North America. They mostly sought cod to be dried and preserved in salt in a form known as "stockfish."

One of the principal English ports involved in the fishing industry was Bristol, but cod could not be imported there legally. Trade in stockfish was under very strict control.

During the greater part of the fifteenth century, most of the stockfish arriving in Bristol was smuggled out of Iceland. The Bristol merchants were therefore always eager to find an alternative supply.

Fishing boats sailing out of Bristol may even have discovered the Grand Banks off Newfoundland, where the seas teemed with codfish, well before John Cabot's first expedition.

If so, they would certainly have kept this information a secret to preserve their profits. If this was the case, they may even have landed somewhere on the east coast of North America.

John Day, for one, believed they did go ashore. He wrote in his recently discovered and now-famous letter describing Cabot's voyage of 1497, which was addressed to an admiral most historians assume must have been Christopher Columbus, "It is considered certain that the cape of the said land was found and discovered in the past by the men from Bristowe [Bristol]. . . ."

But it could even be that the English were not the only Europeans to reach these parts.

COPIOUS COD

In an expedition that set out in about 1472, a Portuguese explorer, Gaspar Corte-Real, is thought to have sailed as far as the Grand Banks. He was rewarded by the King of Portugal with the Governorship of the Azores for having found "the land of the codfish."

None of this diminishes John Cabot's reputation as an explorer. In any event, he personally never claimed to have discovered North America. Like everyone else of the time who knew of his voyage, he thought he had landed in Asia.

Where, then, on the continent of Asia, did Cabot believe he had landed? He did not think he had found the elusive and legendary island of "Brasil" (not to be confused with the South American country we now know as Brazil) that had long intrigued sailors. Instead, he thought he had stumbled across an entirely new island.

In addition to cod, Cabot and his crew, as well as generations of fishermen following in their wake, must have found giant marine life in the region of the Grand Banks.

Cabot must have used a gangplank like the one shown in this fifteenth-century image (*above*) when boarding and disembarking.

DID YOU KNOW?

According to a variety of sources, explorers from any of a number of nations from Europe and beyond may have reached North America before Cabot, including the Chinese, the Vikings, the Carthaginians, the Irish, and the Jews. We will probably never know for sure.

Centuries ago, for religious reasons, about one-third of the year was deemed "meatless" by Christians, so there was a huge demand for fish. When Cabot came across rich fishing grounds off Newfoundland, he was widely praised. His discovery of such plentiful cod eventually led to the settlement of Newfoundland by Europeans more than a century later.

The fishing of cod around the Grand Banks peaked in about 1886. Some was sold locally by street vendors, much was exported, and a large amount reached England, Cabot's adopted home. Just over one hundred years later, however, overfishing took its toll.

This island, he thought, lay just off the east coast of Asia, probably somewhere well to the north of Marco Polo's Cathay. How wrong he was!

The land Cabot had seen and walked upon in the expedition of 1497 was first called the "New Isle." Then, by the early seventeenth century, it became known simply as Newfoundland Island. The shortened form of Newfoundland is the name it bears to this day as one of the ten provinces of modern Canada.

No spices or silks were ever brought back to England by Cabot, but huge quantities of fish, particularly cod, fetched a good price and were potentially just as profitable.

The enormous numbers of fish to be caught around the area of Grand Banks off Newfoundland were soon common knowledge.

Cabot is even said to have sworn that cod were so plentiful off the coast of Newfoundland that they sometimes blocked the way of his ship.

READY MARKETS

Before long, English fishing vessels sailing out of Bristol were joined by ships from Portugal, France, and Spain. Fishermen from these countries regularly filled their ships' holds with huge shoals, or schools, for the market back home. On a single day in 1542, sixty fishing boats are recorded as having sailed for the Grand Banks from just one French port, Rouen.

A rock found at Grates Cove in eastern Newfoundland is said to have borne John Cabot's name, but it disappeared in the mid-twentieth century. Once considered by some to be a genuine relic marking Cabot's presence, it is now presumed to have been a fake.

Meanwhile, a number of European adventurers were determined to explore the territory that lay to the west of Newfoundland, and Henry VII gave permission for further voyages.

> ❝ *If ever there was a fish made to endure, it is the Atlantic cod. . . . But it has among its predators man, an openmouthed species greedier than the cod.* ❞
>
> FROM COD: BIOGRAPHY OF THE FISH THAT CHANGED THE WORLD BY MARK KURLANSKY

In 1501, for example, a group of mariners and merchants from Bristol were asked to sail across the Atlantic and annex for England any lands they might find that were, to quote the royal decree, "unknown to all Christians."

They returned safely and sailed again the following year, this time returning with three Algonquin Indians who fascinated the King and were allowed to live at court.

In 1524, Giovanni da Verrazzano, Italian by birth, explored the east coast of North America for France. Jacques Cartier sailed ten years later and discovered the Gulf of St. Lawrence. Then, landing to the north of Newfoundland in 1583, Sir Humfrey Gilbert once again formally claimed the region for the English crown.

SETTLING DOWN

The London and Bristol Company, which had been established to develop the fishing trade, tried founding settlements in Newfoundland during the early seventeenth century, but they were not successful because of the region's thin soil and harsh climate. In time, however, the exploitation of the region's fine timber resources and a buoyant local fishing industry led to the settlement of Newfoundland.

A LASTING LEGACY?

Cabot's discovery of the fishing grounds of the Grand Banks was to provide a good living for thousands of people over hundreds of years. We now know that the cold Labrador current in that area merges with the far warmer Gulf Stream to provide an ideal environment for the growth of plankton, on which fish, such as herring and cod, love to feed. The Grand Banks' cod were so plentiful that no one before the late twentieth century would ever have dreamed that the area might eventually become severely overfished. But this is precisely what happened within five hundred years. Finally, in 1992, in an attempt to give the ocean's stocks a period of time to recover, legislation was introduced to prohibit any fishing of cod throughout the region. The law remains in force.

STEALING HIS THUNDER

John Cabot achieved an enormous amount in his lifetime. But his son, Sebastian, disrespectful of his father's memory, tried to take much of the glory for himself.

When he landed in Newfoundland, John Cabot could not have imagined he was setting foot on soil that would later fly the flag as a province of the vast country known as Canada. Most historians doubt that his son Sebastian deserved any of the credit.

This painting (*right*) shows ships leaving Spain for the east coast of North America in 1498, the same year Cabot disappeared during a voyage from Bristol on behalf of England. No doubt the Castilian crown had heard of John Cabot's discovery by then. They may have wished they had originally agreed to sponsor his proposed voyage. By this time, they were probably eager to benefit as much as possible from his success.

In medieval times, the sons of sailors usually followed in their fathers' footsteps. Indeed, John Cabot's three sons were specifically named in the letters patent granted by King Henry VII. But how well liked and trusted was Sebastian? Did he actually sail with his father in 1497? The governors of important

London guilds thought little of him. "We think it . . . unwise to risk five ships . . . on the word of . . . Sebastian, who has never been there himself, even if he reports lots of things he heard his father . . . speak of in the past," they wrote to the King concerning another voyage.

> **He sails not surely that sails by another man's compass.**
>
> THE GOVERNORS OF TWO LONDON GUILDS, IN A LETTER TO KING HENRY VIII, 1521, WITH REFERENCE TO THE CLAIMS OF SEBASTIAN CABOT

Sebastian Cabot seems to have been prone to adding details to accounts purely for dramatic effect or to gain influence and prestige. Peter Martyr, an Italian at the Spanish court who compiled the first history of the New World, recorded that Sebastian claimed the Newfoundland cod swam in huge shoals right to the shore, where they fed on the leaves of overhanging trees. According to Sebastian, bears then rushed into the shallow water to surround the fish.

These were not just youthful fantasies, either. At about the age of 70, Sebastian even told the explorer Jacques Cartier that he had made a voyage to Florida, which was not true.

What did Sebastian Cabot actually achieve? He tried to find a Northwest Passage to Asia in 1508, but he failed, according to most historians. Then, during the period from 1525 to 1528, acting for Spain, he set sail around the world on the route taken by Ferdinand Magellan, but he only reached South America's River Plate.

Yet he undoubtedly had a way with words, like many confidence tricksters. He took pains to gain influence in the right circles, which is how he succeeded in being granted pensions by both Spain and England. However, these two sources of income were finally stopped in 1557, shortly before he is thought to have died. He also left a map, dated 1544, that clearly showed the Gulf of St. Lawrence, Canada.

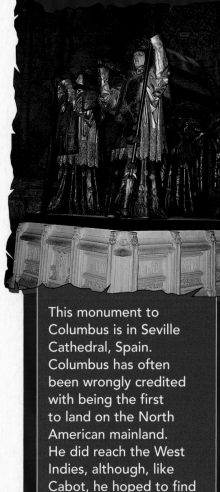

This monument to Columbus is in Seville Cathedral, Spain. Columbus has often been wrongly credited with being the first to land on the North American mainland. He did reach the West Indies, although, like Cabot, he hoped to find a new route to Cathay.

This portrait is thought to be of Sebastian, son of John Cabot, in his later years. No one knows how or where either of them died or whether they sailed together, as Sebastian claimed.

The time of the *Matthew*'s arrival in 1497 — 5 A.M. on June 24 — is marked on the map. This may have been based on hearsay rather than participation in the voyage because he seems to have gotten the point of landfall wrong!

There were those, though, who found him good humored, generous, and entertaining. In 1556, at the age of 74, according to one chronicler who was about to embark on an expedition, "Master [meaning the commander of the ship] Cabot gave to the poor most liberal alms, wishing them to pray for the good fortune and prosperous success of the *Serchthrift* . . . and made me and them that were in the company great cheer . . . he entered into the dance himself, among the rest of the young and lusty. . . ."

In old age, Sebastian's mind may have started to wander. He is said to have boasted on his death bed that he found out about longitude by divine revelation. He must have remained somewhat shrewd, however, because in his later years, he arranged to have a portrait painted. The original disappeared, but we know from copies that it showed him using a pair of dividers and that a Latin inscription appeared in the top left corner. Translated, it read, "Portrait of Sebastian Cabot, Englishman, son of John Cabot, knight of Venice, First Discoverer of Newfoundland under King Henry VII of England." The clever wording makes readers wonder whether father or son deserves the credit!

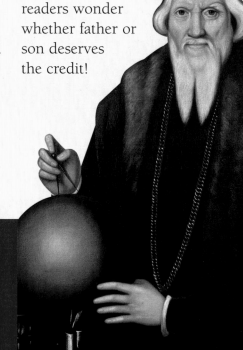

Cabot's second son, Sebastian, stole his father's thunder and later produced this map (*above*) of North and South America. The best that can be said of him is that he was economical with the truth.

This detail showing Sebastian Cabot with a globe and pair of dividers (*right*) is taken from a copy of a painting that was destroyed by fire in the nineteenth century. The original painting featured an inscription (*above left*) in its top left corner. It is thought that Sebastian Cabot deliberately chose the ambiguous wording so it would imply that he was the one who first discovered Newfoundland.

FOR FURTHER DISCUSSION

Many aspects of John Cabot's travels are thought to be controversial and therefore open to debate. The following questions can be used to guide classroom discussion.

1 Do you think that John Cabot could have succeeded in setting sail without the help of the merchants of Bristol?

2 How did England benefit at the time from Cabot's voyages even though he did not reach his intended destination, the Orient?

3 What sort of man was King Henry VII of England? Why do you think he offered Cabot the letters patent that he needed?

4 Do you think that explorers should ever have been allowed to set out on expeditions without the authority of the leader of the country?

5 What sort of qualities were necessary for a sailor in the fifteenth century?

6 If you had to create a monument for John Cabot, where would you place it, and what would it be like?

7 How likely do you think it is that John Cabot and some or all of his crew survived their final expedition of 1498? If so, what might have happened to them, and where might they have settled?

8 Why do you think Cabot sailed with a fleet of five ships in 1498?

9 Who do you think were most helpful to John Cabot's ambitions, and were these ambitions fulfilled?

10 In your opinion, did Cabot leave a greater legacy to the world than he might have left if he had found a westerly route to the Orient?

11 Why were the newly discovered fishing grounds so important to England?

12 If you had been one of the family of Cabot or of his crew back home in Bristol, what would have been your main concerns while they were at sea?

13 Do you think that Sebastian Cabot was loyal to his father?

14 What evidence is there that John Cabot excelled as a sea captain?

15 Was Cabot's main motive in setting out in 1497 the discovery of new lands?

16 Why do you think King Henry VII of England specifically refused to allow John Cabot to sail south from Bristol?

17 What do you think would make a suitable epitaph for John Cabot?

MAJOR WORLD EVENTS

When European interest in exploration of distant lands was at a high point, it was not only curiosity that fueled these expeditions. The discovery of new and faster sea routes to the Orient for trading purposes and a thirst for gold, as well as the spreading of the Christian religion, also came into play.

Find out about some of the major voyages (*right*) made by fifteenth- and sixteenth-century sailors.

■ **1492** Columbus sailed to the Caribbean while searching for a westerly route to Cathay.

■ **1497-1499** Portuguese explorer Vasco da Gama discovered the sea route from Europe to India by way of Africa's Cape of Good Hope.

Cabot rivaled his contemporary Columbus, whose fleet is shown (*above*).

■ **1500** Pedro Alvares Cabral discovered Brazil on the mainland of South America and claimed it for the King of Portugal, Manuel I.

■ **1508** Sebastian, son of John Cabot, sailed across the Atlantic in search of a northern passage to Cathay and may have reached Hudson Bay.

■ **1513** Ponce de León discovered Florida while searching for the legendary Fountain of Youth, said to bring immortality to anyone bathing in it.

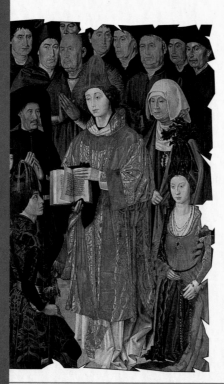

Although he was not a sailor, Henry the Navigator (*left*) sponsored several fifteenth-century Portuguese expeditions.

OVER THE YEARS

- A deep pink rose is named after John Cabot.

- Newfoundland has a Cabot Lake, a Cabot Point, and three Cabot Islands.

No paintings of Cabot exist from his time. This modern portrait was based on a description of him as genial and a skilled seafarer.

- John Cabot University is in Rome.

- Cabot is said to have named a groundhog he found on landing in Newfoundland *Marmota Caboto robustica* after himself. Newfoundlanders and other North Americans celebrate Ground Hog Day on February 2.

- A statue of John Cabot by sculptor Hans Melis outside the Confederation Building in St. John's, Newfoundland, was unveiled in 1971.

- Cabot Tower was built in 1897 at Signal Hill, St. John's, Newfoundland, to mark the four-hundredth anniversary of Cabot's 1497 expedition.

- The Cabot Trail on Cape Breton Island is known for its great beauty.

- In Newfoundland, postage stamps were issued in 1897 to mark the four-hundredth anniversary of Cabot's 1497 voyage.

- At the U.S. Capitol in Washington, D.C., four wreathed panels feature portrait busts of explorers Christopher Columbus, Sir Walter Raleigh, René Robert Cavelier Sieur de La Salle, and John Cabot.

- The replica of the *Matthew*, built to sail to Newfoundland to mark the five-hundredth anniversary of John Cabot's 1497 voyage, rests in Bristol harbor, England. It can be boarded and sometimes takes passengers on short voyages so they can experience life aboard a fifteenth-century ship. Another full-scale replica of Cabot's ship is in Bonavista harbor, Canada.

Born with an Italian name that was anglicized on his arrival in England, John Cabot was certainly among the greatest mariners of his time. His ancestors were probably sailors, too, because his family name signifies someone who sails along the coast.

Cabot's successful 1497 voyage from Bristol, England, to the east coast of North America (which he thought was Cathay) has been marked in many ways (*left*).

GLOSSARY

ambiguous: doubtful or uncertain

argosy: a large merchant ship

armament: weapons

astrolabe: an early scientific instrument that was used to aid navigation by the stars

Azores: a group of islands in the Atlantic Ocean off the west coast of Portugal

barnacles: small, shelled sea creatures that attach to rocks and the underside of ships

bronze: a mixture of copper and tin

canal: an artificial waterway for boats

capstan: a machine for moving or raising heavy weights that consists of a vertical drum that can be rotated and around which cable is turned

Carthaginians: an ancient people from North Africa, near modern Tunis

cartographer: a mapmaker

Cathay: an ancient name for the region that is now known as China

chronometer: an early instrument for measuring time

city-state: an independent city and its territories

comet: an object mostly made of gases and dust that orbits the Sun in an irregular path

commerce: the exchange or buying and selling of products on a large scale, involving transportation from place to place

contaminate: to make unfit for use by the introduction of unwholesome or undesirable elements

cosmopolitan: composed of people or elements from all or many parts of the world

diesel: a type of oil used as fuel

dignitaries: people who hold positions of dignity and honor

epitaph: a brief statement of remembrance for a person who has died

equator: an imaginary horizontal line around the center of Earth

expedition: a journey undertaken for a specific purpose

exploitation: an act of making productive use of something, such as resources

floes: masses of ice in the ocean

furled: rolled up

gangplank: a device along which passengers and crew walk to board or leave a ship

gondola: a canal boat, usually specific to Venice

guild: a medieval association of merchants or craftsmen

Gulf Stream: a warm current in the Atlantic Ocean that flows from the Gulf of Mexico northeast along the U.S. coast and on to Europe

hatch: an opening on a ship's deck

hold: the interior of a ship below decks

horizon: an imaginary line in the distance between the sky and Earth

hourglass: a medieval device for measuring time

hull: the frame of a ship

illiterate: unable to read or write.

Islam: the Muslim faith

keel: a structure along the length of the bottom of a ship

keelhauling: a punishment in which a culprit is hauled under the keel of a ship

knots: a measurement of the speed of ships

lateen: relating to a rig with a triangular sail

latitude: distance north or south of the equator

letters patent: documents from medieval English royalty granting certain rights

longitude: distance east or west of an imaginary vertical line, such as that passing through Greenwich, London, England, measured in degrees

maritime: of the sea

Mecca: the holy city of Muslims, located in what is now Saudi Arabia

medieval: of the Middle Ages

Middle Ages: a period of European history from the fifth to the end of the fifteenth century

Muslim: a follower of the religion of Islam, founded by the prophet Mohammed

mutiny: to rebel against discipline or a superior officer

mythical: legendary

nautical: of the sea or ships

omen: a sign of something that might happen

Oriental: belonging to or of the East

plankton: tiny organisms living in water

Polestar: the North Star, used as a guide to navigation in medieval times

Pope: the head of the Roman Catholic Church

pseudonym: an assumed name used to disguise a person's true identity

quadrant: a medieval instrument for calculating a ship's position at sea

replica: a copy

rigging: lines and chains used aboard a ship to support and work the sails and masts

rudder: an instrument for steering a ship

rutter: a ship's log

scaffolding: a system of temporary or movable platforms for workers to stand or sit on when working at a height above the ground

serge: durable woven fabric

superstition: an illogical belief

unfurled: unrolled

Venice: a medieval city-state and a city in what is now Italy

Vikings: ancient seafaring people from north Europe

FOR FURTHER STUDY

BOOKS

Cabot: John Cabot and the Journey to Newfoundland.
Robin S. Doak (Compass Point Books)

The European Rediscovery of America.
Kelly Wittmann (Mason Crest)

John Cabot: The Ongoing Search for a Westward Passage to Asia.
Marian Rengel (Rosen)

John Cabot and the Rediscovery of North America. Charles J. Shields (Chelsea House)

Travels of John and Sebastian Cabot.
Joanne Mattern (Raintree Steck-Vaughn)

VIDEOS

Challenging Geography: Explorers Discover America. (Rainbow Educational Media)

English Explorers. (Schlessinger Media)

The New World Encountered.
(Rainbow Educational Media)

WEB SITES

John and Sebastian Cabot.
www.mariner.org/age/cabot.html

John and Sebastian Cabot.
www.nmm.ac.uk/site/request/setTemplate: singlecontent/contentTypeA/conWebDoc/ contentId/135

John Cabot.
library.thinkquest.org/J002678F/john_cabot. htm?tqskip1=1&tqtime=0426

John Cabot.
www.stemnet.nf.ca/CITE/kiexp.htm

John Cabot.
www.heritage.nf.ca/exploration/cabot.html